Original title:
Why Life Isn't Always a Straight Line

Copyright © 2025 Creative Arts Management OÜ
All rights reserved.

Author: Alexander Thornton
ISBN HARDBACK: 978-1-80566-096-5
ISBN PAPERBACK: 978-1-80566-391-1

Unfinished Symphonies of the Heart

In a world where socks like to flee,
The paths we take aren't always key.
Chasing dreams that roll away,
We laugh at plans that went astray.

Like a sandwich missing its bread,
We stumble forward, hearts widespread.
With every twist and clumsy turn,
The art of life is how we learn.

An ice cream cone on a windy street,
Gets toppling toppings, oh what a feat!
We juggle hopes with bananas in hand,
And dance on dreams we did not plan.

Each wrong turn paints a silly scene,
Where life becomes a comedy, unseen.
With friends who laugh at every slip,
We raise a glass to this wild trip!

The Spiral Stairs of Tomorrow

Round and round on stairs I go,
Wondering where the next step's flow.
With each twist, my plans get tangled,
Like socks that won't stop being wrangled.

I reach for light at the top so bright,
But stumble back, oh what a sight!
My coffee spills, my wig flies off,
I guess I'll take the elevator, scoff!

Waves of Uncertainty

Riding high on a crest of glee,
Then crash! Oh boy, what's happening to me?
The tide brings chaos and drags me under,
With flippers flailing – it's a blunder!

I surf the bumps and dodge the dips,
Like dodging awkward morning quips.
With every swell, I change my mind,
Shockingly, the beach is hard to find!

Trails Less Followed

Through bushes thick and paths unclear,
I ventured forth with zest and cheer.
But oops! A rabbit led me astray,
And now I'm lost – oh, hip-hip hooray!

I tripped o'er roots, fell face-first down,
Now I'm sporting both mud and frown.
But laughter echoes in the trees,
As squirrels giggle and dance with ease!

When the Compass Spins

My compass whirls like a dizzy bird,
Directions lost – oh, how absurd!
North becomes south, and east goes west,
I think I'll just follow the weathered nest.

With each wrong turn, I find a new show,
The world's a stage with a quirky flow.
So here's to laughs and wobbly ways,
As I roam through life's delightful maze!

When Roads Converge

Two paths collide, a clumsy twirl,
Sign says 'left', but here comes a swirl.
I took a step, tripped on my shoelace,
Now I'm dancing in the wrong place!

A fork in the road, I took a chance,
Said yes to sushi at a clown's dance.
I aimed for fortune, got a pie in the face,
Guess life's a circus with a touch of grace!

The Beauty of Intention Gone Awry

I set my goals on a lofty shelf,
But tripped on dreams, and fell on myself.
A smoothie spill on a brand new shirt,
I'll start my diet… after dessert!

Thought I'd bake a cake, so divine,
But mixed salt instead of sugar—oh, fine!
Life's recipe has its quirky blend,
With laughable plots that twist and bend.

Navigating the Uncharted

With a map in hand, I chose to roam,
Got lost in a neighborhood, far from home.
A dog led the way, with style and flair,
Now we're on the hunt for his favorite fare!

My heart wanted Paris, but I ended in Spain,
Sipped coffee under a sun with no rain.
Unexpected sunsets on sandy shores,
Where life spills secrets, and laughter pours.

Unfolding in the Flux

Like origami, I'm folding and creasing,
Plans unwind with each giggle, increasing.
Chasing my shadow, it took a detour,
Turns out I prefer bliss over a chore!

Life jiggles, jives in a silly dance,
Couldn't find my light, but caught a glance.
Turns out the fun is in the mishaps too,
In every wrong turn, there's a new view!

Unpredictable Horizons

Woke up today with a plan in mind,
But the cat knocked my coffee, oh how unkind.
I set out to conquer, to climb every hill,
Only to find that I'm stuck in a spill.

My GPS told me to take a sharp ride,
But instead I found myself in a tide.
Navigating life's map is truly an art,
Especially when you take a wrong turn from the start.

When Plans Go Awry

I meant to cook dinner, gourmet and divine,
But the smoke alarm's laughing, it's making me whine.
The recipe said 'simmer,' I turned up the heat,
Now my lovely stew's a charred, crunchy treat.

I planned to be early, but fate had a role,
The train was delayed, it swallowed my whole.
Instead of the boardroom, I'm late for a show,
Guess it's a good thing I'm just going with flow.

From Shadows to Light

The sun peeked out, chasing shadows away,
But I tripped over shoes at the start of the day.
I stumbled and fumbled, with flair and with style,
Even my mirror could barely keep a smile.

Thought I'd find wisdom in all that I learned,\nYet every wise quote left my brain quite burned.
I can't find the path; I've turned left and right,
But every wrong turn makes for more funny sights.

Ribbons of Experience

Life is a ribbon, tangled and bright,
A dance in the dark, then a skip into light.
One minute I'm soaring, next I'm falling flat,
It's not always serious, just look at my cat!

Tried to be mature with goals set in stone,
But instead I found joy in my ice cream cone.
Each twist and each turn, a giggle resides,
With laughter the compass where humor abides.

The Looping Odyssey

I took a stroll, felt pretty bright,
Then tripped on a shoe, lost my sight.
Round and round, I spun in glee,
A comedy act, oh woe is me!

I chased a squirrel, thought it was great,
It darted off — now I'm running late.
Through twisty paths, I start to roam,
My heart a map, but my feet—oh no!

Against the Grain

I wore my shirt inside out today,
Fashion mistake? Hipster's way!
I took a left when I should've gone right,
Now every street looks like the night.

With toast in one hand, coffee in the other,
I tried to juggle, oh why'd I bother?
Spilled the drink, and to my surprise,
The mug was laughing; what a wise guy!

Roadblocks and Revelations

Found a shortcut on the way to work,
But ended up in a swamp—what a perk!
A frog gave me pointers, quite the sage,
He croaked wisdom, filled with rage.

I built a bridge from a pile of fluff,
Thought it would help; turns out, it's tough.
Fell in the mud, but I laughed instead,
Insurance claim? I'd rather just tread!

Echoes of a Winding Trail

The path ahead twists like a dancer,
I trip and roll, oh what a prancer!
A snail smiles slow as I rush by,
"Hold on," it says, "life's a sly guy."

With every stumble, I sprout a laugh,
The map is wrong, but oh, what a path!
Each turn I make, I find something new,
Maybe my GPS needs a review!

The Beauty Beneath the Curves

In life's grand race, we dash around,
But trip on shoes that don't fit, we've found.
Yet laughter erupts from the falls we take,
As we dance in circles, giggling at fate.

With every twist, a surprise does appear,
A clown with a nose, and that's a cheer!
For every straight path is a snooze, you see,
Curves add the spice; oh, how fun it can be!

Whirlwinds of Thought

Round and round my brain does whirl,
Like a kid on a swing, giving life a twirl.
One moment it's soup, the next it's a pie,
Thoughts ricochet, bounce—oh my, oh my!

I planned to be wise, to stay on the track,
But ended up chasing my own silly quack.
Embracing the chaos, I let out a snort,
For straight lines are boring—pass the popcorn, I court!

Life's Eclipsed Lines

In the dark of night, shadows may sway,
Like a pencil confused, it starts to dismay.
Wobbly and wonky, the outlines do fade,
But here's a plot twist: the fun's in the shade!

Riding a roller coaster of ups and downs,
Who knew clowns throw parties with frowns?
When day meets the night, and they start to blend,
You'll find laughter's the line, the curves it sends!

The Hidden Turn

I thought I had it all mapped out just right,
Yet found a detour that sparked sheer delight.
A squirrel on a skateboard, a cat in a hat,
Life's hidden turns made me giggle and chat!

We're taught to go straight, but oh what a bore,
When loops and backflips open the door.
With every wrong turn, we carve our own lines,
Creating a story that humor defines!

Interstellar Turns

In a galaxy not so far,
Stars twirl like dancing cars.
One moment you're in the groove,
Next, you're trying to make a move.

Space cows drift without a care,
Wormholes lead you anywhere.
Asteroids play tag, oh what a mess,
And aliens ask, "Did you just confess?"

Navigating twists with glee,
In zero gravity, lost is the key.
All systems fail but who needs plans,
When every curve leads to new dance spans?

So strap in tight for the ride ahead,
With laughter and logic, fears you'll shed.
In this cosmic funhouse, take your shot,
For the journey's the prize, forget the plot!

The Tale of a Twisted Branch

Once there grew a mighty tree,
With branches waving wild and free.
One day it sneezed, oh what a sight,
A twisty turn took it in flight!

A squirrel lost his morning nut,
He searched and searched and then got stuck.
With a tumble, flip and airy cheer,
The branches whispered, "No need to fear!"

Rabbits hopped in a zigzag lane,
Chasing sunshine, ignoring the rain.
Upside down in this wild old dance,
Life taught them all to take a chance.

Beneath the boughs, they gathered 'round,
With every loop came laughter, profound.
In the tale of branches, a lesson found,
The funniest roads often confound!

Loops of Joy and Sorrow

Round and round the merry-go-round,
 Life spins fast without a sound.
Sometimes a giggle, sometimes a cry,
 In this circus, we learn to fly.

A jester juggles with zest and flair,
 Slips and trips fill the air.
He tumbles down, but with a grin,
Shakes off the dust, and hops back in.

Friends fall over laughing in rolls,
 Collecting stories, capturing souls.
 Glorious chaos in every cheer,
Bouncing back with each wild tear.

So grab the loop and don't let go,
 Embrace the ebb and every flow.
For in the dance of highs and lows,
Is where the love of laughter grows!

A Cascade of Choices

In a land of forks and tangled paths,
Each step you take creates many laughs.
Pick a door and take a peek,
You never know what turns you'll seek.

Will it rain or will it shine?
Choose the line; the thrill is divine.
The cat's in a hat, the dog wears shoes,
In this world, who can refuse?

From juggling plates to riding bikes,
With funny slips and wild hikes.
Every choice leads somewhere new,
Sometimes silly, sometimes true.

So let's cascade without delay,
With giggles guiding our funny way.
In this whimsical world of ours,
The wackiest choice becomes the stars!

When the Journey Takes a Detour

I thought I knew the way to go,
But then I tripped on a garden gnome.
With a twist and turn, it stole the show,
Now I'm wandering far from home.

I sought to find a quick shortcut,
But ended up in someone's yard.
They raised their brows, and I felt struck,
This unplanned stop hit me quite hard.

Road signs mocked me, how rude they are,
As I zigzagged past a cow on a road.
With every turn, I'm a lost star,
Finding adventure in my heavy load.

Yet, in these bends, laughter awaits,
Glimpses of joy in my funny plight.
Cheers to detours that life creates,
Let's toast to the wrong turn tonight!

Weaving Through the Unknown

I planned a map, so neat and tight,
But fate drew lines like a toddler's art.
Instead of roads, I found a kite,
That took me soaring, a brand new start.

Navigating paths I did not know,
I rolled with tides of whimsy's cheer.
With every turn, I stole the show,
Who knew wrong turns could feel so dear?

Encounters with a duck parade,
Was not the plan I had in mind.
But on this route, I'm sure, I stayed,
Life's quirks are gems that we can find.

So here's to chances, unplanned frolic,
With every twist, there's giggles abound.
In knots we weave, there's nothing solid,
But love and laughter always surround!

Captured in Spiral Moments

Life's a spiral, so it seems,
A loop-de-loop of bumps and grins.
Chasing my dreams, I tripped on beams,
But oh, the joy in all my spins.

Thought I'd glide on a straight path,
But found myself in a merry dance.
With every slip, I felt the laugh,
Embracing chaos, my wild chance.

I sailed a boat made of cotton candy,
Over waves of jello, squishy delight.
With each new turn, the whims get handy,
Who knew detours could feel so right?

So here's to curves, our winding fate,
In spirals of giggles, we find the way.
Each twist and twirl, we celebrate,
In this twisted game, life's a play!

Tides of Deviation

I set my sail for the straight and narrow,
But waves of laughter crashed my bow.
With every twist, I felt like a sparrow,
Gliding through storms, oh wow, oh wow!

Strangers dressed like pirates and jesters,
Joined me on this curious ride.
Each step we took broke all the testers,
And in this chaos, I felt so wide.

Navigating through a kaleidoscope,
With every hiccup that came to light.
Unexpected turns fill me with hope,
Finding laughter in the wildest flight.

So cheers to tides, those playful waves,
As we bobble along this mad spree.
In every swerve, adventure saves,
The heart of life, wild and free!

Forks in the Road: Choices We Make

At every turn we smile wide,
With options galore, we can't decide.
An ice cream cone or broccoli?
We laugh as we dance, oh what could be!

The left says 'bake', the right says 'fry',
Meanwhile, our pants just watch and sigh.
Do we heed the signs or take that leap?
Life's a circus; it's laughable, not deep!

So pack your bags, take chaos as a friend,
Mix up your map; it's fun, not just pretend.
Plant your flag on uncharted ground,
In this wacky world, joy's always around!

With every wrong turn, we do the twist,
In this maze of laughs, you're never missed.
Embrace the forks, the silly detours,
In life's buffet, it's giggles that endures!

The Haphazard Map of Breath

In a world where 'X' marks the fun,
You'll find a twist in every run.
Hopscotch paths with silly rhymes,
Mapping giggles with joyful chimes.

Take a detour, sip on some tea,
The way may curve but let it be.
Between the chuckles, take a breath,
Finding joy is part of the quest!

The road may wiggle, it may flip,
Each bend a chance for a wild trip.
Just like the hiccup after a giggle,
Wobbly paths keep our minds in a wiggle!

So hold on tight, to this playful ride,
With every mishap, let joy abide.
We'll dance through life with tangled grace,
Every twist and turn, a brand new face!

Tangents of the Soul

Life's merry-go-round spins upside down,
We reach for gold, but find a clown.
With every tangent, we've lost our way,
Finding laughter in what led us astray.

Off the beaten path, we chase the fun,
Skipping stones, oh look, we've run!
A carrot or a cupcake, who can choose?
In the great game of life, you just can't lose!

The heart's our GPS, but it's out of whack,
Telling us to turn, but we stay on track.
Riddles and giggles lead us anew,
Through every quirk, we find our view!

So skip along the curvy trails,
With a wink and a laugh, there's no more fails.
In tangents we trust, embrace the folly,
In the waltz of life, we'll be jolly!

Curved Reflections in Still Waters

In ponds of laughter, ripples spread,
Reflecting joy in boatloads ahead.
Each splash a giggle, a twist, a turn,
In the dance of the waves, feel the yearn.

Peering in deeply, the truth's a tease,
Mirrors of folly with smiles that please.
Nothing is straight — it's all a wee bit,
We ride this rollercoaster, we never quit!

The ducks are dancing, a wobbly show,
Life's jokes bounce off in moments that flow.
With every ripple, new stories unfurl,
In still waters of laughter, watch life twirl!

So gather round the pond of play,
Where reflections are fun in every way.
In curved paths, we find our delight,
Embracing the giggles, we take flight!

Patterns of Imperfection

I thought I'd dance, with rhythm sublime,
But tripped on my shoelace, oh what a crime!
The tango turned into a wild jig,
Clumsy feet make a laugh, not a dig.

I tried to bake a cake all unbent,
But flour flew high, it wasn't quite meant.
Eggs on the floor and batter on me,
A masterpiece? More like a comedy.

Packing for trips, I aimed for quite neat,
Yet clothes flew like confetti, what a feat!
Adventures await in chaos and fun,
A suitcase explosion, who's next on the run?

Life's full of curves with laughter inside,
Straight can be boring—let's take a ride!
So bring on the chaos, the giggles, the mess,
After all, in the bumps, we find happiness!

Hurdles and Highroads

I planned a straight dash, with purpose so clear,
But hiccups like squirrels brought snickers and cheer.
Avoiding the puddles, I aimed for dry ground,
But splashed like a dolphin—oh, what a sound!

A casual jog turned into a leap,
Hurdling obstacles that made me go 'eep!'
Over the fence like a graceful gazelle,
Or tumble like meatballs? Only time will tell!

Navigating life is a dizzying race,
Where the finish line keeps changing its place.
I'll skip and I'll hop, no straight route I'll find,
With laughter as fuel, I'm not far behind!

Bring on the bumps, bring on the flops,
For every misstep, more giggling pops.
In this wobbly journey, I gotta confess,
The crooked paths hold the most happiness!

Footprints in the Sand

Walking on beaches, the sun shining bright,
I tripped on a shell—oh, what a sight!
My footprints were zigzags, a wonky design,
Each step a new party, beach trails combine!

Building a castle, I aimed for the sky,
But the tide had a plan, oh me, oh my!
The castles were washed away with a splash,
A sandy surprise, what a fun little crash!

Crabs scurried sideways, I joined in the fun,
Embracing the chaos under the sun.
Life's not a straight path in grains or in sand,
It's jumbled and giggly, perfectly planned!

So let's dance with the waves, let's prance on the shore,
With laughter and footprints who could ask for more?
In every soft imprint, may joy be our guide,
Through twists and through turns, in laughter we glide!

Navigating the Untamed

In jungles of chaos, I ventured with glee,
Got lost with a laugh, like a bumbling bee.
Thought I'd cut through, what a clever plan,
But I tangled in vines, like a clumsy young man!

The map said "This way!" but oh, what a jest,
I ended up face to face with a nest.
The squirrels threw acorns, a nutty parade,
I waved in surrender—was that a charade?

Taking a shortcut? That's surely a myth,
For the path I took led to a wild twist.
A dance with the branches, a twirl in the air,
If you tumble and fall, you might as well share!

With every misstep, new stories take flight,
The best tales are woven from chaos and light.
So here's to the journey, the wild and the grand,
In the uncharted places, let laughter expand!

The Jigsaw of Life's Design

Pieces scatter all around,
Some fit well, others confound.
Edges sharp, colors awry,
Who knew puzzles could make us cry?

Flip that piece, oh what a mess!
In the end, it's all just guess.
A picture's formed, yet still amiss,
Maybe this isn't what I wished?

A corner here, a blob of pie,
I swear that cow's not in the sky.
Laughing with friends, we try again,
Life's better with a dash of zen!

So here we sit on carpeted ground,
Joy in chaos, laughter abound.
Each lost piece still brings us cheer,
Let's toast to jigsaws, my dear!

Paths of Nonconformity

In a world where straight lines gleam,
I twirled and danced, oh what a dream!
Followed signs that said 'take a right',
But found myself lost last night!

Meandering streets with quirky bends,
Making friends with squirrels and hens.
A detour's charm, a thrill that's grand,
Who knew wrong turns could be so planned?

Off the beaten path I roam,
In gardens where no one calls home.
Each step brings giggles, unexpected,
Somehow I've lost all that's respected!

So here I prance, a happy fool,
Life's less about the straight, more the drool.
Take that fork in a curvy lane,
And laugh at rules like they're just a game!

Through Thorny Thickets

Wandered through the thorny brush,
Thought I'd find a fancy rush.
But oh, those prickles shook my plan,
Guess I should've brought a fan!

Twisted paths where daisies cling,
Beware of the vine that likes to sing.
Pancakes for breakfast? Wrong way, friend!
Found a raccoon, my new best friend!

Navigating nature's silly traps,
I tripped and fell, took a few naps.
Yet each bruise brings a hearty laugh,
Guess I'm really not on a straight path!

Emerging with a wild new style,
They call me the thicket child.
Though some may fear these tangled vines,
Here I stand, and sip my wines!

The Art of Indirect Routes

Took a shortcut that led to a moat,
Riddled with ducks, still in my coat.
Thought I'd win the race to the end,
But hello! There's one quacky friend!

Maps are useless when fun's the aim,
In circles I go, but who's to blame?
So many lanes that twist and shout,
I'll take the scenic, amidst the clout!

A road sign points to fun and glee,
Navigational chaos, do you see?
Missed my destination, well that's just grand,
Let's stop for ice cream, can you understand?

So map your life with lots of flair,
The straightest route? Who needs that scare?
With laughter and joy, I'll always know,
The best adventures are in the flow!

A Tangle of Directions

I thought I'd take a stroll today,
A simple path, no need to sway.
But left and right, I lost my way,
Now I'm in a field of hay!

I waved to cows, they looked confused,
Their moos, a laugh at my contused.
I asked for help, they just stood still,
Trusting Google Maps was not a thrill!

I turned around and found a stream,
Uh-oh! Mismatched paths, not my dream.
I jumped a log, fell with a splash,
Now I'm wet, but oh, what a crash!

So here I sit, a grin on my face,
Life's a circus, not a race.
With each wrong turn, a chuckle grows,
Guess it's how the randomness flows!

Serpentine Steps

I planned a jog around the block,
But tripped on shoes that wouldn't lock.
My left foot went, my right said, 'No!'
Down I tumbled, who knew? Oh no!

Around the corner, a squirrel paused,
He flicked his tail, I was just awed.
With dizzy spins, I joined the chase,
Wasn't running! What a wild race!

Downhill I zigged, up I zagged,
While my coffee cup also lagged.
Each twist a dance, each turn a joke,
In my own world, yes, I bespoke!

At last, I stopped, with breathless glee,
Thought running was just plain old me.
But here I am, swirling and twirled,
Life's like a game—a silly world!

The Uncharted Route

I grabbed my maps and set to roam,
The world ahead, not far from home.
Each street I took began to weave,
More paths than a magician's sleeve!

With every turn came unexpected sights,
A dancing cat and bubble fights.
I found a tree that looked like a hat,
With birds perched high—all chitchat!

I waved goodbye to my planned detour,
Found lemonade stands rather than a cure.
A parade popped up, all color and cheer,
Who needs a destination when fun's so near?

So here's a thought on roads unplanned,
Stick to your laughs, let chaos expand.
Maps are just guides, but joy's the quest,
Dance through the world, it's for the best!

Embracing the Detours

On a sunny morn, I set to explore,
A trail I thought, but oh, there's more!
I bumped into a carnival queen,
With glitter and sweets, oh, what a scene!

I meant to wander to the local store,
But found a frog doing much more.
He hopped and danced like a whirling top,
Caught in a rhythm, he just wouldn't stop!

A pizza truck beckoned, 'Get in line!'
Wait, that's not my plan—oh, how divine!
With every bite, I forgot my aim,
Each twist in life feels like a game!

So here I laugh at roads once laid,
Life's a jigsaw, not a charade.
Through each mishap, I've come to see,
Every detour hums with glee!

Fragments of the Unexpected

I planned a trip to sunny shores,
But ended up in a store for drawers.
The GPS said, "Turn right on cue!"
Turns out, it wasn't even true!

I took a step and tripped on air,
Landed face-first in a big old chair.
Now I'm a meme, it's quite a laugh,
Life sure knows how to change the path!

A coffee spill splatted on my shoes,
They say it's luck—what a funny ruse!
With every bend, there's humor found,
Life's little jokes keep spinning round!

Yet here I am, still on this ride,
With mismatched socks, I take it in stride.
For every twist and turn I face,
I find a chuckle in life's embrace.

Chasing Shadows in the Mist

I woke this morn to find a cat,
Sitting on my hat—a friendly brat.
I chased it down, a wild pursuit,
Only to slip, for the floor was a hoot!

The coffee pot's now a fountain grand,
With espresso rain falling on my hand.
As shadows dance in morning light,
I laugh at chaos—what a sight!

I saw a squirrel with acorn flair,
Running a race with the neighbor's hair.
Who'd guess the antics softly cease,
When laughter fills the air with peace?

Through swirling mists, I roam anew,
Chasing quirks that life bids me to do.
If shadows linger, I won't stall,
For every giggle makes me stand tall.

The Nonlinear Dance of Time

Tick-tock said the clock, quite ill-timed,
Danced with a cow, oh how it chimed!
Pasta in the air, what a delicious toss,
My meal is a twirl, with sauce as the boss!

In socks that don't match, I skip and glide,
Through puddles like planets—what a wild ride!
Each tick is a jig, each tock is a spin,
Time's quite a dancer, let chaos begin!

I once planned my day with care and might,
But the dog chased a butterfly into the night.
Now plans are just suggestions, a merry prank,
For time's fancy footwork leaves me blank!

So here's to delays and moments undone,
Where laughter's the partner, stress comes undone.
In the grand ballet of fate and rhyme,
I twirl through the folly, embracing the clime.

Bends in the Fabric of Fate

I wore my shirt backward, what a fine sight,
A fashion faux pas, I made it my rite.
With mismatched buttons, I strut with glee,
A model of chaos, can't you see?

A trip to the park turned into a chase,
After a duck who thought it could race!
I stumbled and fell, but with a grand flair,
Life's little blunders, I'm happy to share!

I baked a cake, but forgot the eggs,
Ended up with cookies atop some pegs.
Sweet surprises come with each twist and bend,
In the recipe of life, laughter's the trend!

So here's to the flaws that make us real,
To bends in the fabric—what a steal!
With giggles and grins, we take the ride,
For life's strange patterns bring joy with pride.

The Kaleidoscope of Reality

Colors twist and turn with glee,
Shapes that none can clearly see.
Life's a dance on disco dots,
Some days bubbly, others not!

In a loop, we twirl and spin,
Chasing laughter, chasing sin.
Each corner holds a quirky sight,
A clown that's trying to take flight!

Laughter bursting like bright balloons,
Silly moments like cartoon cartoons.
The world's a jigsaw, odd and wide,
With giggles hiding in each stride!

Twists and turns with every glance,
We waddle forth, a silly dance.
So grab a friend, and let it fly,
In this crazy fun, we'll learn to try!

Steps on a Twisted Path

Stumble here, a hop and skip,
Watch your step, avoid the trip.
Life's a path with puddles round,
And mysteries that can't be found.

With quirky stones beneath our feet,
Wobbling forward, can't be beat!
A crooked sign that points to fun,
Who needs straight when we can run?

Up a hill and down we roll,
Landing smack on a friendly mole.
Life's a maze with giggly cheers,
Laughing out the passing years!

So dance along this bumpy track,
With every stumble, we won't look back.
The joy is in the silly sway,
Embrace your steps, come laugh and play!

Ripples in the Stream of Existence

Waves of wobbles, splashes bright,
Life's a circus, what a sight!
Float along on rubber ducks,
In this stream, there's lots of luck.

Turtles racing, fish that smile,
Swirling dreams in a goofy style.
Jump the ripples, ride the tide,
In these currents, we'll abide!

One day calm, the next a splash,
Life gives surprises in a flash.
Swim with giggles, float with glee,
Strange fish sing a silly spree!

So grab your boat, let laughter sail,
Through river bends where giggles trail.
With every ripple, let out a cheer,
In this wavy world, we have no fear!

Scribbles of the Brave

Crayon colors on the page,
Doodles dancing, full of rage.
Lines that zig and lines that zag,
Chaos wrapped in a happy bag.

A dragon roars, a cat can fly,
A silly pig, oh my oh my!
Life's a scribble, wild and free,
Artful madness, come and see!

Each twist and turn, a story told,
With every stroke, we brave the bold.
Erase the flaws, let laughter ring,
In this mess, we find the swing!

So let's embrace the scribbled fun,
A wacky journey just begun.
With crayons strong, in colors bright,
We paint our path with pure delight!

A Symphony of Turns

In the orchestra, notes collide,
Trumpets honk, violins slide.
A cat on a piano, oh what a sight,
Music's a dance, both wrong and right.

Cabbages roll across the floor,
While cows break in, asking for more.
The conductor slips, age-old mistake,
Laughter rises, make no mistake.

Symphonies twist in comedic glee,
Life is a jest, come laugh with me.
Where banjos play with saxophones,
And nobody claims to know the tones.

Yet through this wild, nutty show,
We find joy in the chaos, you know.
With giggles bright in every turn,
Every misstep, still more to learn.

The Curved Canvas of Experience

With splashes bold and swirls galore,
Paintbrushes dance, colors implore.
A canvas flipped upside down,
A masterpiece? Or a circus clown?

Sunshine purple, oceans green,
Doodles and dribbles, sights unseen.
A palette spills, colors collide,
The artist laughs, oh what a ride!

Brushstrokes zigzag, up and down,
As the paint drips, oh what a frown!
Yet in the mess, a story hides,
Each curve and line a wild ride.

In swirls of chaos, laughter brews,
For art's not bound by straight-line views.
With every twist the heart does soar,
That quirky canvas we all adore.

Hills and Valleys of Being

In hills so steep, a tumble starts,
Rolling down, but where's the cart?
A donkey brays, a bike goes slow,
Life's little quirks put on a show.

The valleys hug like soft, warm bread,
Where hopes lie low, the dreams get fed.
But up we go, and down we slide,
With giggles loud, we're filled with pride.

In every dip, a joke awaits,
With gravity pulling, oh how it fates.
A snowman's hat flies far and wide,
As we burst forth with laughter inside.

So grab your kite, hold on real tight,
Through all these bends, we find delight.
For on this path of hills and bends,
We dance with joy, and joy transcends.

The Spiral of Days

Each day a twist, a dizzy spin,
Like hamsters running, we race and grin.
Coffee flies as spoons take flight,
Morning hugs feel just right.

Around we go, the clock ticks loud,
Waves of people, a bustling crowd.
Umbrellas turn in the wild wind,
Life's a game where we pretend.

A potato rolls, a dog barks back,
Our paths may veer, but never lack.
With each new turn, surprises await,
Even burnt toast can be first-rate.

So spiral on, let laughter lead,
In every twirl, we plant a seed.
For in this dance, each loop we find,
Life's swirling fun, never maligned.

Halfway Up the Hill

I thought I'd take a simple path,
But tripped on my own math.
The shortcut turned a twisty route,
I laughed so hard, I couldn't scoot.

Up the hill, my snack rolled down,
I chased it, wore a goofy frown.
With every step, my shoes would squeak,
Is life a joke or just unique?

I met a goat that seemed quite wise,
He winked at me, and ate fries.
His motto, 'Slow and steady wins',
But he was chasing after bins.

So here I am, at halfway's quest,
With no idea what's for the best.
But laughter lines my crooked way,
And keeps the silly fears at bay.

The Echoing Curves of Experience

I tried to take a straightforward route,
But ended up in a chicken suit.
The map said left, but my gut said right,
Now I dance with clucking delight.

Up ahead, a sign said 'Detour',
I shrugged and pressed, can't be a bore.
Each curve a giggle, each bump a laugh,
Who needs a straight line, just take a gaff?

With every twist, I found a friend,
A guy with jokes, the fun won't end.
His puns, like speed bumps, made me cringe,
But life's a laugh, so I'll binge!

So here's to routes that twist and twirl,
To ups and downs that make me whirl.
Experience echoes, loud and clear,
In every giggle, love, and cheer.

Scratched and Worn Maps

My map is scratched, coffee-stained,
It leads to roads I've never gained.
I thought I'd find the straightest path,
But detours sparked a fit of laughs.

There's a note that says, 'Beware of dogs!',
Yet I met them all, in muddy fogs.
Each bark a riddle, each woof a clue,
What's a trip without a furry crew?

I sailed through puddles, jumped some grass,
With every wrong turn, I'd come to pass.
Life's not mapped, it's chaos divine,
With every twist, we redefine.

So here I roam, uncharted land,
Worn maps in hand, as fate had planned.
Laughter guides me, it's clear and fine,
In this scrambled maze, life's still a sign!

Driftwood Dreams by the Shore

I built a castle of driftwood bright,
But the tide thought that was quite a sight.
With every wave, my dreams would shift,
What a fun twist, what a lovely gift!

I tried to catch a passing star,
But ended up with a jelly jar.
Filled with thoughts and glittery schemes,
Life laughs with us in silly dreams.

Sand between my toes, I dance around,
With every fall, a giggle's found.
The shore, it curves, it bends, it plays,
So I keep twirling through the maze.

With driftwood dreams washed up ashore,
Every 'Oh no!' opens a door.
The humor in waves, rushing and free,
Is the best kind of life, don't you agree?

The Flawed Map of Meaning

My map says go left, but I veer to the right,
A squirrel leaps by, what a curious sight!
I swerved for a donut, oh what a delight,
Now I'm lost in a maze that's not quite contrite.

Where's the finish line? I keep missing my turn,
With each wrong direction, just more to learn.
The path isn't clear, but I'm starting to yearn,
For another surprise, oh, I'm beginning to churn.

The X marks a spot that's a café, not gold,
In a world full of stories, there's joy to behold.
Each wrong turn I take, feels like fate has been sold,
And laughter erupts, every moment's retold.

So here's to the twists; they lead to the fun,
With friends in mischief, we'll run and we'll run.
Embrace the confusion; let chaos outrun,
For life's crazy journey has only begun.

Wandering Through Whims

I started my day with a list and a pen,
But a butterfly flits, grabbed my focus again.
I followed it swiftly, to learn where it's been,
Through candy floss clouds, where the wild dreams begin.

A detour for laughter is always in season,
With giggles and wiggles, what's wrong with that reason?

Instead of the gym, I'll have French fries with cheese on,
And dance with the moon, till I'm puffin' and wheezing.

Maps drawn in crayon are washed out by time,
My plans on the fridge now are simply a rhyme.
With friends on this ride, every step's sublime,
Through whimsy and wonder, we plan and we climb.

So here's to the paths that go nowhere at night,
The laughter we find when we're lost with delight.
Together we wander, our joy taking flight,
In this whimsical journey, it all feels so right.

No Straight Lines to Home

I thought I was clever with a route in my head,
But detours appeared, turned my plans into dread.
A stroll through the park where laughter is spread,
And now I'm just chasing my own feet instead.

The GPS laughs as I circle around,
Climbed up on a fence, then fell to the ground.
With pigeons as witnesses, life's joy can be found,
Each tumble and giggle, a love truly profound.

The twists and the turns lead to places unknown,
With new friends I make over ice cream they'd thrown.
We chase after rainbows, not caring we've blown,
A chance meeting serves the best stories I've grown.

So let's raise a glass to the roads that we roam,
For wild is the journey that leads us back home.
In every misstep, new memories we comb,
For life as it happens, it's never alone.

Patterns in the Chaos

There's a roadmap of giggles where mishaps run free,
A stumble turns into a sweet cup of tea.
What looks like a mess, makes a grand tapestry,
With patterns of chaos embracing you and me.

I tripped on a dog, who decided to play,
As I danced through the puddles, come laugh at my sway.

With hiccups and hurdles, my plans went astray,
But joy in the chaos is here to stay.

The world spins around, with surprises galore,
One day I'm on top, then I'm flat on the floor.
Yet this wiggly journey is never a bore,
In the maze of our lives, we just keep wanting more.

So here's to the patterns that we can't foresee,
A life full of laughter and curious glee.
For woven among us, in each twist we see,
Is the art of existing, just let it be free.

Curves in the Pathway

In a world that's oddly bent,
I took a stroll, my back was spent.
With every twist and every turn,
I found new things that made me learn.

I tripped on roots and danced on stones,
Chased a raccoon who stole my cones.
The path ahead—a winding spree,
Who knew life's fun could look like me?

Each corner hides a silly shock,
Like clowns appearing from a clock.
With wobbly wheels and giggles too,
I'm learning laughs are meant for you.

So grab your hat and hold on tight,
Embrace the goofy, see the light.
With every bump and every fall,
Life's a ride, let's have a ball!

Twists of Fate

Once thought I'd be a chef so fine,
But ended up with a puppy and a line.
My soufflé fell, my cake did flop,
Now it's dog treats I must chop.

I tried to dance like all the pros,
But tripped on shoes that came and goes.
The crowd all laughed, I took a bow,
And joined the clowns—I'm wiser now.

A job I thought was really cool,
Turned out to be a swimming pool.
With rubber ducks and water fights,
I learned that work can bring delights.

So heed the signs that twist and twine,
Sometimes you're lost, it's just divine.
Each random twist that fate has spun,
Is full of joy—we're not quite done!

The Zigzag Journey

With every step, I zig and zag,
Like a lost bee with a funny tag.
I hopped on buses—missed my stop,
Ran into llamas, heard them bop.

The road was long, a noodle path,
I slipped on mud, oh what a laugh!
Found a hat that fit a cat,
I thought "This journey isn't flat!"

Played leapfrog with a jumping frog,
Rode a unicycle through the bog.
Every twist spills giggles wide,
Life's got humor—what a ride!

So let the zigzag lead the way,
To places bright where we can play.
With laughter as our joyful guide,
We'll dance through life, side by side!

Beyond the Expected Turn

Plan A was neat, all nice and straight,
But life had plans, oh isn't fate great?
I set my course for coffee bliss,
Ended up in a cat's abyss.

Met a mime in a funky hat,
Tried to chat—it was no chit-chat.
We laughed with gestures, danced in place,
Life's silly turns are full of grace.

A detour led to pie in hand,
Onward I went, feeling so grand.
Each wobble brought a smile so wide,
Life's circuitous is on my side.

So here's to turns we didn't see,
To quirky paths that set us free.
Beyond the plans we thought we drew,
Life's making fun—let's join the crew!

Braided Paths of Choices

In a world of twists and bends,
Decision-making never ends.
You pick a route, then take a turn,
Forget the map! It's fun to learn.

Like spaghetti on a plate,
Life's a mix, isn't it great?
You think you know just where to go,
But then you trip on what you know.

Winding roads with shiny signs,
Glimpse of joy in silly times.
One day you're dancing in the rain,
Next, you're trapped in pizza chains.

So let's embrace the silly path,
And chuckle at the aftermath.
For every bump, there's laughter bright,
In this crazy, joyful flight!

Vortex of Change

Round and round the whirlwind spins,
A rollercoaster with no wins.
One minute you're on cloud nine,
Next, it's socks without a line.

Life's a dance with silly moves,
Like misfit socks that never groove.
You chase the breeze that won't stay put,
In a game of hopscotch, who's tooot?

Life offers pies with crusts all cracked,
And tiles galore, so many stacked.
You think you've landed on solid ground,
But lo and behold, you're upside down!

Yet in this joyful wild ballet,
We spin and twirl our cares away.
For every drip and silly splat,
We savor each chaotic chat!

The Spiral of Living

Twists and spirals like a game,
Sometimes it feels a little lame.
You plan your course, then lose control,
Jumping through hoops that take their toll.

On a merry-go-round of fate,
Clutching dreams that can't wait.
You reach for stars, but grab a shoe,
What next? A dance on a BBQ?

Life's a spiral made for laughs,
With upside-down, mismatched halves.
You think you've found the winning plot,
But find yourself in a pickle pot!

So laugh and swirl, embrace the jest,
For every mess, we're truly blessed.
In this delightful carefree ride,
Let's spin and giggle, side by side!

Errant Whispers of the Wind

The wind whispers secrets, quite absurd,
Chasing squirrels, flying like a bird.
One moment brave, the next a clown,
Like slipping on a banana down!

In the forest of what should be,
You'll find a frog that's keen to flee.
You chase your dreams, while they just smile,
Then hop away to their own style.

Branches divert in silly schemes,
Chasing butterflies, not your dreams.
You think of plans all neat and true,
Then get sidetracked by a petting zoo!

So when the wind tells tales so wild,
Laugh it off and be like a child.
For in this dance of errant flight,
Every twist makes living bright!

The Art of Meandering

A squirrel crossed my path with flair,
I thought I'd follow, but it was a dare.
Chased it down a street, into a tree,
Now I'm lost, oh where could I be?

Life's a dance, with steps gone wrong,
Waltzing sideways to a silly song.
Turn left for ice cream, right for a snack,
Do a little twirl, then head right back.

The road is bumpy, with speed bumps galore,
Hit one too fast, now I want to explore.
My GPS said, "Recalculating,"
But I'm more interested in what's awaiting.

A cat in a hat, a frog on a bike,
Unexpected guests, oh what a hike!
Yet in this chaos, joy intertwines,
Embrace the twists; it all defines.

Waves of Uncertainty

Riding the waves of a cotton candy sky,
I thought I'd surf but learned to fly.
Fell off the board into a bowl of fruit,
Bananas and berries, oh how cute!

Plans like a sandcastle, washed by the tide,
A crab stole my lunch; it couldn't abide.
Lifesaver floaties didn't quite work,
I splashed and I flailed; that's how I lurk.

Navigating currents with an inflatable duck,
Floating along, hoping not to get stuck.
The beach umbrella swirls in a funny way,
Knocked out my sandwich; oh, what a day!

But laughter's a breeze that fills the air,
With every wave, I'm stripped of despair.
And as I paddle right into a wall,
I find that I'm having the best time of all.

Curves in the Journey

A little detour, oh what a twist,
Found a shortcut I just couldn't resist.
But the road led me to a petting zoo,
Where I made friends with a goat named Lou.

Life's a rollercoaster, up and down I go,
With each twist and turn, it puts on a show.
I tried to take notes on my looping spree,
Then I ended up lost with a clown named Steve.

"Hold tight!" shouted the driver, all filled with glee,
But the map flipped over and blinded me.
Was I going left or playing hopscotch?
I bounced like a ball, then heard a loud squawk.

Yet in the curves, I found the delight,
With each misstep, I learned to take flight.
So here's to the paths that don't go as planned,
Twists and turns make the moments so grand.

The Tangle of Existence

I tripped on my shoelace, fell in a puddle,
Next thing I knew, I was in a huddle.
The ducks quacked loudly; they thought it was fun,
While I just wished I could find some sun.

Existence is like spaghetti, all tangled and neat,
With twists and with turns, it can't be discreet.
Just as I pondered the sauce and the bake,
A stray cat jumped in—what a big mistake!

"Grab my forks!" yelled my friend, and we did,
Finding the forks was like a treasure bid.
Between laughter and mess, we shared a good meal,
The topsy-turvy path became part of the deal.

So here's to the mess," we waved in delight,
At the wild, juicy chaos that feels so right.
For in every tangle, we each find a thread,
A funny odd story that's barely been said.

Winding Paths of Destiny

A snail thought he could race,
But ended up in a slow embrace.
With each twist and mishap he found,
The garden was round and quite profound.

The bird on a bike tried to soar,
But crashed into a squirrel galore.
Who knew acorns could move that fast?
Is this life's joke, are we all outclassed?

Unraveled Threads of Time

The cat chased her own tail in a loop,
While dogs cheered her on from the stoop.
Every spin made her dizzy and light,
The audience howled with pure delight.

In the kitchen, the chef made a mess,
Mixing sugar with salt, what a guess!
His soufflé now resembled a brick,
Yet laughter echoed, what a fun trick!

Twists and Turns of Tomorrow

A jester juggled pies with great flair,
But one hit him squarely—oh what a scare!
With whipped cream masking his frowning face,
He laughed it off, still in the race.

The rabbit wore shoes and missed the bus,
Said he'd hop there, it's not a fuss.
Yet he tripped on his laces, what bad luck!
Now he's late for a dinner with a duck!

The Maze of Moments

In a maze full of mirrors, I lost my way,
I thought I saw my twin—a clever play!
But he pointed left, then right at me,
While I grinned back, 'We both disagree!'

The hedgehog searched for the end of the path,
Only to step into a puddle, oh wrath!
With soggy quills, he waddled around,
And laughter erupted; the joke was profound!

Labyrinth of Choices

In the grocery store, I lose my way,
Aisles like mazes make me sway.
Should I grab the pickles or the jam?
I'm not quite sure, so I just stand.

The map of life has its twists and bends,
Like a cat who thinks string's her friend.
I take a step—oh, what a mess!
But laughter's the best, I must confess.

What road to take, I ponder still,
Do I go left or just uphill?
With every choice, a chuckle grows,
Like socks that vanish, who even knows?

Embrace the chaos, let it unfold,
In every tale, there's laughter untold.
As I navigate with random flair,
I might end up with a rubber duck there!

Unfolding in Unexpected Ways

Woke up one day, thought I was wise,
But my shoes were mismatched—what a surprise!
Out the door and into a puddle,
Oh great, now I've made quite the muddle!

Plans set in stone, till the weather rebels,
A picnic in rain? Well, that's how it gels.
Sandwiches soggy, but spirits aren't low,
We dance and we laugh in the downpour's glow.

Life's like a kite caught in a tree,
The strings pulled by fate, yet wild and free.
A twist here, a twirl there, what's left to expect?
Sometimes a detour ends up architect!

So here's to the paths that swerve and slide,
With friends by my side, I'll take the ride.
A laugh, a snack, and a splash of cheer,
Who knew uncertain could be so dear?

Ebb and Flow

Like waves on the beach, our plans shift and sway,
I thought I'd be rich, but hey, that's okay!
The tide brings surprises, like lost keys in sand,
I just keep on searching, or maybe I'll stand!

Sometimes a current can pull me away,
From the path I had charted, oh what a day!
But float like a cork, I learn to surf,
When laughter is plenty, it's all good turf!

A rollercoaster life with its loops and spins,
I stumble and tumble, but somehow I win.
With every high, a giggle or two,
Turns out the bumps are the best part of you!

So cheers to the flow, the give and the take,
In this zany world, there's no need to break.
With humor as buoy, I'm sailing through glee,
The sea of absurd is my cup of tea!

The Beauty of the Unknown

What's around the corner, nobody knows,
Could be a garden, or just more snow!
I step with glee, a treasure awaits,
Or maybe a joke about clumsy plates!

The universe chuckles, its mysteries grand,
Like socks that get lost in a loveable band.
I expect a parade, and it's just a cat,
But oh, what a sight, imagine that!

Each twist and turn, a comic delight,
I bring my own snacks for a whimsical bite.
With stumbles and fumbles, I take a quick spin,
And burst out in laughter; oh, where to begin?

So here's to the path that's foggy and wide,
With odd little creatures that dance by my side.
The unknown's the spice, a giggle's the goal,
And life's greatest stories bring joy to the soul!

The Road Less Traveled

With maps in hand, we set the scene,
But who knew grass could look so green?
A shortcut here, a turn gone wild,
Lost in laughter, like a child.

The GPS begged, 'Recalculate!'
But we just shrugged and felt so great.
Each twist and turn, a brand-new ride,
Together we laughed, what a fun glide!

Whispers of Divergence

Paths diverge like silly jokes,
One leads to cows, the other to folks.
A detour here, a snack stop there,
We stumble upon a tiny fair!

With every wrong move, a story grows,
Dance with squirrels and pose with crows.
Life's a mix of fumbles and glee,
Whoever knew wrong turns could be free?

Edges and Turns

Round the bend, what a surprise,
A pizza shop under funny skies!
We thought we'd find a towering bridge,
Instead, it's pasta and a fridge!

With every edge, a chance to grin,
Like playing tag with fate and sin.
So here we are, not quite on track,
But who needs straight when you've got snack?

The Mosaic of Moments

Life's a quilt of mismatched seams,
Painted with laughter, woven dreams.
A splash of chaos, a dip of cheer,
We find connections everywhere near.

In the mess of turns, we dance and spin,
Collecting memories, stocked to the brim.
So let's toast to roads that twist and bend,
For every new route, there's more fun to send!

Fractured Footprints

In the mud, my shoe got stuck,
A dance of soles, oh what bad luck!
One step forward, two steps back,
Like my cat, who can't find the snack.

Sidewalk cracks hold secrets deep,
Where squirrels plot while others sleep.
A tumble here, a trip and spin,
It's a circus act, let the fun begin!

Rainy days bring puddle splashes,
With every jump, my patience crashes.
Umbrella flips as winds take flight,
I'm just a kite, lost in delight!

Even maps can lead astray,
Taking routes in a wobbly way.
But in each turn, a chuckle lies,
Life's just a jest in a silly disguise.

Serpentine Shadows

Creeping slowly, like a snail,
I zigzag up and down the trail.
A shadow dances, bends, and sways,
As I forget the path I trace.

My morning coffee spills, oh dear,
No straight lines in my java here!
Each sip a twist, and there I go,
A smile grows, oh what a show!

Umbrella flips, I'm caught in rain,
Jumping puddles, oh the pain!
But laughter echoes, fills the street,
As I perform my clumsy feat.

Life's a jigsaw, pieces stray,
Finding edges that won't obey.
Yet in the chaos, joy we find,
For laughter's path is unconfined.

Echoes of Uneven Roads

Treading lightly on rocky ground,
Bumps and ridges all around.
With every step, a funny hop,
Like I'm auditioning for a flip-flop.

Maps can lie; GPS too,
Why's the shortcut always askew?
I make a left, then a right, then a spin,
Waving to clouds, letting the fun begin.

At the corner, a dog in a hat,
Looks more dignified than I, how 'bout that?
We share a glance, a moment's pause,
Together debating life's silly flaws.

A road that twists is never bland,
Each curve is crafted by a playful hand.
With laughter's echo guiding the way,
Adventure calls, so let's obey!

Chasing the Horizon's Bend

I ran so fast, lost track of time,
Chasing shadows, spinning in rhyme.
The horizon giggles, just out of sight,
Teasing my steps in the fading light.

Round the corner, what do I find?
A garden gnome, ever so blind.
He stands with pride, but looks quite confused,
As I whirl past, utterly bemused.

Clouds pile up, a storm in bloom,
Yet I'm laughing, in my own little room.
A paper plane sails to the stars,
Drawing a map of whimsical scars.

As I chase each twist and turn,
Life's little lessons, so much to learn.
In each dip and rise, laughter is penned,
For every journey finds a bend.

Intersections of the Heart

Two paths meet, oh what a sight,
One's dressed in pink, the other's in fright.
They both say, 'Hey, you look like a ball!'
And trip on their laces, then stumble and fall.

Left turns and rights, it's a dance of fate,
Like a blindfolded chef trying to plate.
The map in my head says, 'Go green or go blue!'
I grin at the chaos, what else can I do?

Chasing the sunset in flip-flops and quirks,
Get lost in a maze of inquisitive smirks.
My compass spins wildly, no north in the game,
But laughter is gold, and that's never lame.

So here's to the forks, the pies and the bends,
Who knew little detours could lead to new friends?
A tentative heart takes leaps with a laugh,
Navigating the madness, I'll take any path!

The Mosaic of Misadventure

A canvas splattered in colors so bold,
Each brushstroke a tale waiting to be told.
Upside-down rainbows, a cat with a hat,
I painted my troubles, they look good like that!

Tripped on a banana at the grocery store,
Tried to impress but fell hard on the floor.
The snack aisle chuckled at my epic fail,
I laughed till I cried; what a curious tale!

Piecing together this jigsaw of glee,
With mismatched socks, what a sight to see!
Adventure awaits in the strangest of places,
Like falling in love with a pair of fat laces.

Embrace all the hiccups, the wobbly paths,
With laughter and giggles instead of the wraths.
Life's a mosaic, painted with quirks,
Let's dance in the madness, it totally works!

The Story Beneath the Surface

Beneath the calm waters, lurk mischief and fun,
A fish wears a bowtie, thinks he's the one.
He poses for selfies with a wink and a grin,
But forgets he's a fish; let's check if he can swim!

The duck on a tricycle, a sight to behold,
Still balancing feathers for a price yet untold.
He weaves through the park, all wobbly and whirled,
What's next, a pig flying? Now that'd be wild!

Life's undercurrents are twisty and sly,
Like a circus of turtles just learning to fly.
I marvel at chaos that bubbles and swirls,
When seaweed's a sassy fashion choice for mer-girls.

So dive in the waters, find humor in strife,
It's all about laughter, the essence of life.
With stories like these that forever amuse,
Beneath the surface, you'll always find blues!

A Journey in Paradox

I packed my bags, oh what a mess,
To find my way home, I must first guess.
The map's upside down; I'm lost in the park,
I thought I'd find treasure, just found a remark.

A road made of rubber and sliding on rain,
Thought I'd take shortcuts, but we're all on the train.
With signs saying 'left' but I'm going the right,
I'll dance with the wrongs till the morning light!

A beautiful riddle, wrapped up in a joke,
As I fumble my way through a puff of white smoke.
Each bump and each detour, a story to share,
With a wink and a nod, I'm stripped of despair.

So here's to the paradox, the fun and the flip,
Where cats ride on scooters, and snacks start to zip.
In a world of bemusement, let whimsy take flight,
For the path of confusion is my favorite delight!

Meandering Through the Unseen

Woke up this morning, socks don't match,
Lost my keys, oh what a catch!
Coffee spills on my shirt, oh my,
Off to work — but don't ask me why!

Walking straight, I hit a tree,
Laughing at fate, it's just so free.
Pavement cracks like a grin so wide,
Chasing my thoughts like I'm on a slide.

Maps can't help with the roads I take,
Sidewalks twist like a giant snake.
Directions? I'd call that a joke,
Missing my exit as the GPS spoke.

Yet here I am, with stories to tell,
Rolling through chaos, just like a bell.
Life's not a line, it's a wiggly path,
Join in the dance, embrace the aftermath.

The Dance of Unexpected Journeys

I packed my bags for a neat little trip,
But forgot my wallet — time to flip!
Hotels booked, but all were fake,
Couch-surfing now, what a funky break!

A train delayed, I start to grin,
Chatting with strangers, letting fun in.
My suitcase rolls off to who knows where,
Lost in the wild, but I don't care!

At dinner, my salad's a sight to see,
Lettuce flies like it's chasing me!
Spaghetti's dancing on my plate,
Who knew food could have such fate?

So let's twirl through life, all zig and zag,
We're lost on purpose, no time to brag.
Take a wrong turn? Let out a laugh!
Every detour's another great path!

Zigzagging Through the Stars

With a compass in hand, I start a quest,
To find that star, I think was best.
But instead of straight, my path's a swirl,
Dancing through planets, oh what a whirl!

Each step I take feels like a tease,
Gravitational pull? Just a breeze!
I tripped over comets, slid down a moon,
Floating along to an offbeat tune.

I asked a rock for directions, you see,
But it just sat there, staring at me.
Constellations giggled, lighting the skies,
As I zigzagged through their silly replies.

So here's the scoop, as I zoom around,
Life's a bit loony, but that's how it's found.
Stars know the way when we take the dive,
Search for the wobbles; that's how we thrive!

Labyrinths of Heart and Mind

In the maze of thoughts, I dance around,
Tripped on a feeling, what have I found?
Chasing my dreams through corridors bright,
Lost in the echoes, day turns to night.

A heart's little game, it pulls and it tugs,
Sent me for coffee with wintery bugs.
Plans that I drew on a napkin, oh dear,
They scribble away like they've all disappeared!

Puzzles and riddles in my own head,
Thought I detected the path that I tread.
But every wrong turn's a giggle, you see,
For the heart likes to play hide and seek with me!

So here's to the twists, the knots in my mind,
Each loop is a lesson, each feint fell behind.
In this crazy maze, make a colorful mess,
There's fun in the chaos, a joyful confess!

www.ingramcontent.com/pod-product-compliance
Lightning Source LLC
Chambersburg PA
CBHW051701160426
43209CB00004B/975